Discover Your Spiritual Genius

THE BEGINNER'S GUIDE TO KNOWING IT ALL

Discover Your Spiritual Genius

Dr. kac young

Your Shortcut to a
Spiritually Fulfilled Life

Design and typesetting by
John Cole GRAPHIC DESIGNER, Santa Fe, New Mexico

SAN number: 850-6876

SECOND PRINTING. August 2004
THIRD PRINTING. April 2006

This book is dedicated to three
amazing women,
with my deepest appreciation.

To Sister Ruth Marie Gibbons who was the
first person in my educational life to be a
"Yes." Her inspiration and dedication
to excellence propelled me into zest-filled
life experiences that
have enriched me beyond limits.

To Terry Cole-Whittaker who continues to
delight, teach and inspire as one of the
greatest "Ah-has" of all times.

To Marlene Morris, my Minister, my teacher,
my encourager, my muse, my grace,
my audience and my living treasure.

ACKNOWLEDGEMENTS

The following people have given enormous inspiration to my life and hence, this book. My deepest gratitude to:

Jerry Luedders

Geraldine Jones — Peggy Jones

Danny L. Jones — Tracy Abbott Cook

Ralph Ventura — Pamela Ventura

Jo Head — Godfamily Wells

Carolyn Lombardo — Robert E. Parkinson

Ernest Holmes — Thaddeus Golus

Patricia Mischell — Pat Watson

George Weinberg — Don Skeoch

Sylver Terrace Lane — Jabez

The Naughty Fairy — Jerome

Christina Tillotson — Carole Tashel

DEFINITION OF A

SPIRITUAL GENIUS

We should not separate Life from living, Spirit from matter, nor Divine Principle from a Universal Creation. God is "All in all." That is, God IS, and is in everything. The gardener finds a divine idea concealed in the seed; loosed into action this idea produces a plant. The geologist finds the imprint of invisible forces in the rock. The scientist finds an energy concealed in the atom, and the Spiritual Genius *discloses an intuitive knowledge, which can be accounted for only on the theory that we lie in "the lap of an Infinite Intelligence." So close is the union of creation with the Creator, that it is impossible to say where one begins and the other leaves off.*

— Ernest Holmes, *The Science of Mind*

CONTENTS

CHAPTER ONE

Spiritual Genius Revealed

Do not get me wrong. There is no implied claim here to be THE Spiritual Genius or an authority of any sort. There is only a claim to being *a* Spiritual Genius. Just like everyone else on the planet, I possess a self-styled, self-activated Spiritual Genius inside of me. I am my very own unique version of *a* Spiritual Genius and so are you. If you get that point right here, right now, you can stop reading. If you are curious or confused, or better yet, *stirred up* and want to know more, then tally ho! Read on, my fellow searcher.

The ideas contained herein are for the adventurer. It is for you if you are a restless soul who seeks more of everything you already have, are willing to do a little bit of work, some internal assessment and are more than willing to get your hands a bit dirty in order to clean up old ways of thinking and living that no longer serve your golden dream. This book is *NOT* for the timid or those who just want to pay lip service to transformation or who want somebody else to do the work for them. If you are truly ready to be *a* Spiritual Genius, then let's not waste another second. If you want a pity party and someone to hold your hand and watch politely as you tear up and dab your eyes for the umpteenth time, this book is *not* for you. This is a shortcut to real personal power with tips from one who has walked across rocky terrain, received a fair share of bruising, slammed a few doors (and as a result can't go back there anymore), and who unabashedly celebrates all of it. If you feel that life is too short to keep whining and walking in circles, then this is the book for you. Whether you want a serious jumpstart or a minor tune up, keep reading. Change into your spiritual work clothes, and let's roll!

A little background always helps to clarify exactly what we are talking about. We're consciously creating a way of life. A life that is filled with joy, confidence, wisdom, generosity, abundance, prosperity, love, attraction, fun, health and an unseverable connection to *God/Spirit/Universe/Yaweh*

/Father/Mother/Energy/Creation/You-Name-It/Call-It-What-or-Who-You-Will/Perfection/Cosmos/Dalai Lama/Hello Dolly/or Fred.

This is the most desirable life on earth because in it *all* the pieces fit together. Genuine fulfillment and happiness are experienced *ALL* the time! "Arrrrrrgh! Impossible!" you say, "Life is hard, I'm unhappy a lot of the time." "Okay," says the Spiritual Genius. The path to becoming *a* Spiritual Genius does not happen overnight. It evolves out of the cumulative experiences in your life. You can become *a* Spiritual Genius even if you have been abused, wasted, addicted, hurt, betrayed, slapped, praised, celebrated, punched, loved or spoiled rotten. You can be *a* Spiritual Genius if you have won an Academy Award, or even if you haven't. It's so natural that it may appear intimidating. Truth is, the only way I know that I am *a* Spiritual Genius is because a very spiritual person I know and love told me so. She had nothing to gain or lose by telling me that. She and I had actually just come from a meeting where we had to convey some unpleasant things to a well-meaning group of people.

Although our styles of communication differed, together we moved the group in the direction we wanted them to go, knowing full well our vision contained the highest good and the best outcome for everyone involved. Neither of us had a personal agenda, so our differing approaches worked harmoniously. Following that meeting, she dubbed me *a* Spiritual Genius. Holy Crow! "But what does this mean?" I asked myself, "and what am I supposed to do with this information?"

When I returned home that night and told the sweet love of my life what I'd been called, there was no laughter. Instead there was a great big smile and some delighted giggles mixed with twinkling eyes. "Oh dear! This can't be good," I thought. When your partner doesn't laugh that means *Truth* is present. It's time to pay attention. If there had been a smirk, or a guffaw, there would not be this book. I would have recoiled in horror. Nary a laugh was heard. I figured I better pay attention. Spiritual Genius, huh! I began to ponder.

Our partners are invaluable barometers to the reality of life. They have seen us without makeup and in both the sunlight and the shadows of life's days. They know who we are whether we have on our chiffon party dress or are bare-ass naked with *all* the warts showing. They've seen every side, every depth and every mood. They have seen our tough rhino skins and through our fragile, vulnerable veils. When they can still look us in the eye, connect deeply with us and then beam a loving grin, you know there is undeniable *Truth* present. And thus Spiritual Genius was born. The work here is to speak the truth and let all the little secrets out of the bag so others might profit and gain spiritual fulfillment.

My dear friend, Geraldine Jones, who first spoke the words to me, "*You* are a Spiritual Genius," didn't read it in any text, she didn't find it scribbled on a wall, she simply experienced it. She witnessed the warrior and the delicate infant all in one. To her they are as compatible as salt and pepper. What she saw in me as Spiritual Genius was actually inside of her. She only recognized that part of herself reflected back to her through me. When you come right down to it, *she* is the teacher. It isn't me. I'm just the conduit. Secretly, she is completely entertained by the fact that she can get me to stick my neck out and put this concept on paper and out into the world, while she stays safely at home and tends her posies. I can hear her laughter now as she slaps her thigh and says, *"You go girl!"* So, if this book strikes a chord with anyone who reads it and awakens a dormant inner Spiritual Genius, then she was right. And you can tell her yourself. Remember her name, Geraldine Jones. You'll be hearing a lot more about Geraldine later in this book. But for now, let's get back to our main subject: YOU!

CHAPTER TWO

Your Bottom Line

This book is all about ideas and actions that assist you to reach inside to awaken, stir and cultivate the Spiritual Genius within yourself. You don't need to give your life up, unless you want to. You don't need to follow anyone or give away your power, unless you want to. You don't need to move to a different city. You don't need to stop eating chocolate. You don't need to quit your job, and you don't have to change one iota about who you are or where you've been unless you want to. You only have to actively consider where you are going and how it is you are going about it. This book is about the bottom line of spiritual living.

If you want to release your dormant Spiritual Genius it is an ironclad requirement that you be true to yourself, listen to your own internal feedback and follow some principles that are as old as dirt. Personally it took me many walks on many roads and serious travel time on hundreds of freeway systems before I found my path. This book can show you how to be happy with yourself, how to make peace with your parents and your past, how to get up every morning filled with joy, how to go to sleep every night knowing you lived another successful day, and how to feel that you wouldn't trade a minute of what you've been through or where you're headed for all the sand in Sinai.

You wouldn't have been drawn to this book if something weren't already knocking on your door. Lessons appear when the student is ready. They always do, without fail. So if you are a true seeker, your footpath and your journey will unfold. It may even surprise you how easily, effortlessly and smoothly it shows itself to you. The truth about being a Spiritual Genius is really easy, once you "get it."

There are only two requisites for becoming or being a Spiritual Genius. Chapters Three and Four give you these two non-negotiable requirements. One is about being wise versus being smart, and the other is about getting over yourself.

As Julia Cameron says, "Leap and the net will appear." Are you ready? Then let's jump in.

CHAPTER THREE

You Don't Have to Be Smart, But You Do Have to Be Wise.

To have wisdom you need to look at your life as a series of gifts strung together like beads on a necklace. Your "beads" are the incidents and experiences in your life that give you the ability to "look" at who you truly are.

We are not judged by who we are, but by who we are perceived to be. — John F. Kennedy

The size, shape and appearance of your necklace is the greatest accessory you wear in the world every day. Is yours made of precious gems that sparkle in the light? Or is yours dirty and dingy and hidden inside your clothes so no one can see it? The necklace of life is the sum total of where you've been and the roads you have traveled. It is to be worn and celebrated like the Crown jewels of England, even if they seem to contain darkness or negative memories. There is nothing to be ashamed of. "Yeah, but what about _____? And, _____?" you protest. There is *nothing* to fear. The beads are not your personal Scarlet Letter. You owe it to yourself to be proud of your beads. You earned them! If you don't particularly like the beads you have gathered so far, you can change the kind of beads you accumulate in the future.

So you say, "But what about my hurts? What about what 'they' did to me? What about my wounds and my badges of shame and blame and stolen fame? I can't give those up. They are *meeeeee*." The Spiritual Genius says, "Great! If that's how you really feel, salute them! Applaud them. Appreciate them. Thank them. Bless them." That's the way you get them shiny. Your beads are the results of your experiences, and those experiences have given you the wide field of choices from which you have fashioned each and every one. "But I didn't have any control of *that* situation," you cry. "They did it *to* me." The Spiritual Genius says, "This may be true. But no one ever controlled how you *felt* about it and what you took away from the situation." "But, but,

but," you cry out in defense. Hang on. We'll cover feelings in a minute.

If you absolutely can't wait, The Spiritual Genius directs you to two books: *Man's Search For Meaning* by Viktor E. Frankl, and *A Day in the Life of Ivan Denisovich* by Alexander Solzhenitsyn. The first book portrays the courage and wisdom of a man living in a concentration camp during World War II. He found his own joy and survived, despite horrific, painful and grotesque circumstances. He could easily have said, "Look what they are doing to me," but he didn't. Read what he has to say. The second book is about a man in a Siberian prison camp who developed miraculous gratitude in heinous circumstances. Real people, real stories, and they can get you out of the whineyard in an instant by telling you their truth.

Are you feeling a little bombarded? Has the comfort carpet been ripped out from under you? Are you looking for a softer message? Are you ready to not only *put* this book down, but *throw* it out the window? Great! It's working then. You have been shaken out of your comfort zone. You have been alerted to your need for compassion and absolution. YIPPEEEE! This is time to celebrate. "How is this possible? Are you nuts?" Hold on to those feelings. Remember, this is a *shortcut*. You bought the book because it says so on the cover. You wanted a quick fix. So here it is. This is the spiritual path without the anesthetic. Come on. You're doing great. Suck it up. You wanted the fast track. Keep reading.

Let's return to the subject of feelings. *Yes*, our feelings are important. Indeed, feelings are just sweet messengers of our humanity that let us know what's really going on inside us. Picture them as little Fed Ex guys delivering presents to our conscious mind sent directly up from our heart. The package we receive simply brings us what we have spiritually ordered. "Please sign here on this line for the gift you ordered." How nice would that be? If we can get to a point where our feelings are nothing more than little taps on the shoulder reminding us what we ordered instead of devastating boulders ruining our days/weeks/months/years, then we have accomplished one of the steps toward being a Spiritual Genius.

"But my feelings are my feelings. I am entitled to my feelings. They are important to me. No one has ever understood how I feel," you say, and why? Because you've heard it on so many talk shows. Well, a whole slew of bartenders have heard the same thing too. Over and over, for decades. The Spiritual Genius says, "You're right! Of course you are! Feelings are fabulous, have them! Acknowledge them, but don't let them run the show. They are not in charge, *you* are."

"But, but, but," you say, "No one understands me." Oh balls! Of course they do. We *ALL* understand you. We've all been hurt, betrayed, slapped, kicked, left behind, not chosen, and we've all been praised, thanked, kissed, loved and sung "Happy Birthday" to, or not. We've all not been asked to dance at the hop. We've all been a little overweight, or a lot overweight and we've all not measured up to some standard somewhere, even if it was just a ride at Disneyland with a height requirement we couldn't meet, or failing every test in high school including Driver's Ed. Nobody is spared these experiences. Some people just take them more seriously than necessary. Even Wolfgang Puck had a prize soufflé collapse.

Here's what you do with your feelings: *Practice them.* Go ahead and have them. But set a timer. At the end of five minutes, change your feelings. "What? I can't do that! What if I'm crying because I'm sad, because someone really, really hurt me?" Do you want to be a

Spiritual Genius, or not? Okay, then you stop crying after five minutes. Just stop. You may have to do this exercise a few times, but stop you must. Once you've stopped crying/ screaming/ranting/being sad, then *think* of how you *want* to feel. If you don't *want* to be crying, then change what you are thinking about and shift your feeling completely. "But I can't stop. I have to cry it out! I've been hurt. I need time to cry/rant/pound my fist/crawl under the covers." Oh dear. The truth is you need the time only if you *think* you do.

What if you decided five minutes was plenty of time to recover? What if five minutes was all the precious life-time you were willing to waste on this particular *reaction* you are having to one of life's many situations? What if you decided that you would allow yourself to feel what you are feeling so thoroughly and completely in five minutes there was no longer a need beyond that to dwell on something that happened in the past, even if it was only six minutes ago? What if you had that much power and control over your *feelings* that you only let them have the reins for five minutes? After that, what if you took hold of the reins and steered your life where you wanted it to go instead of being dragged on your face in the muck for miles (years) and miles (even more years) by a team of runaway horses? What if you took hold of those reins, even if it meant chafing your hands a bit and steered the team in the direction you truly wanted to go? What if that were the case? What would your life look like? Isn't there something else you'd rather be doing than sobbing your eyes out?

Okay, we *know* someone did you wrong! We know that, otherwise you wouldn't be crying. But do you want your life to be all about the song, *Please Mister Please, Don't Play B-17*? If you can just get to the point where you allow the five minutes to be full of all the emotion you have and be authentic and genuine about it, you can get over almost anything in five minutes. Replace that old song with any new song on the jukebox you choose. Change the music. And if the old song still bugs you, leave that place and find a new dance floor!

But what about all those talk shows? What about all the therapists out there who want you to feel your feelings and bring them out to be analyzed and dissected? The Spiritual Genius says, "We were all born with the ability to feel. Then we were taught to think. It's what we think that causes our feelings to change, not the reverse." "But it's not that easy," you plead. In the beginning it may *seem* difficult. But so is just about everything new when we first try to learn it. Were you instantly successful the first time you rode a bike? How about skating? Driving? Cooking? Ever burn a pot roast?

The first time is always in the discomfort zone because you're not competent at the task yet. Give yourself a break. Allow yourself to learn this new skill. A Spiritual Genius isn't made in a day, but it can be born overnight. You must master your feeling-based emotional life if you are to be spiritually fulfilled. Hang in there with this technique, and you can master it. You'll be an expert in no time. It's like any learned skill. Practice.

"But it isn't fair, I've spent all this money on therapy just so I could have the right to have my feelings and now you tell me this?" Yeah! Pay attention! Feelings are fabulous. We're just putting the kitchen timer on them so *we* can tell *them* how long they can hang out/on. Then we pat them on the po-po and send them off to bed until the next time they have some-thing to tell us. It's all about positioning. You don't have to put them away forever. Or as the old joke goes: "How do you get to Carnegie Hall? Practice! Practice. Practice!"

Okay, okay, so for the bigger life challenges you can allow yourself ten minutes. See the following chart for the time you are allowed to dwell on the situations of life. Remember, the time you waste on negative feelings is time taken away from the joy you could be experiencing. This is not designed to limit you, but to *FREE* you to have more fun, more joy and more of the good feelings in life.

Situations of Life	Time Allowed for feelings In Minutes
Spanked	5
Ignored	3
Rejected	5
Betrayed	10
Lost ball game	5
Lost Parent	10 at a time, 2-year limit
Divorced	10 at a time, 1-year limit (less if there are children involved)
Moved	10
Lied to	5
Stolen from	5 (for each $10,000 value)
Duped	5
Dumped	5 (under age twenty; add 5 for each decade)
Fired	5
Hurt	5-10 depends on how/where/who
Beaten*	Contact the
Sexually Assaulted*	appropriate
Raped *	authority

*   Societal law governs these. Take the time you need to pursue your legal rights and to attain the state of spiritual forgiveness. These three supersede all time limits. Just don't take too long, so you can get on with the rest of your life. See Exercise #2, "Creative Ways..." in Chapter Nine for an experience in forgiveness. Once you have forgiven, you have ten minutes to exercise your feelings.

You are allowed to "extend" the time if you need to. Look at the timer as your own personal alarm clock with a snooze feature. If you need more time, take it. But remember, the "snooze alarm" lets you have only four or five more minutes before signaling "time's up" and you need to get on with your life. Use the snooze alarm if you absolutely need it, but don't let it lull you back into sleep. Be aware that the extra time you use up is five minutes you'll never get back. Be sure you have something really valuable to show for it.

Now give this next exercise a try. Please, do yourself a favor. Stop resisting. Sit back. Quit wiggling. Close your eyes. It takes only five minutes!

Exercise: Begin to think about someone/something/someplace that has strong emotions or *feelings* attached to it. It doesn't matter if this was a happy or sad experience. Just close your eyes and have the feelings. *Set a timer*. After five minutes, listen to the ringer and stop what you are thinking, as if you had just awakened from a sound sleep. Immediately think about something else. Imagine you were dreaming, and immediately think of how late you are to get to work, or of all the things you have to do that day. Your feelings instantly switched from the dream-state into reality. Here and now, repeat the exercise and recreate that same experience. Change your thoughts. How did your feelings change?

If you have successfully done the exercise this time, you can do it anytime and anyplace to alter your experience. Take the timer with you. The next time you are stuck in traffic, allow yourself to feel the rage/anger/frustration/fear/impatience. Set the timer and then after five minutes allow yourself to think of something else, maybe that trip to Hawaii you crave, and let *those* feelings surface. You'll begin to experience how easily you can shift your feelings because of what you are thinking. This technique will come in handy next time you are faced with a life situation that ignites powerful feelings. You will see how *you* are in control and not the *feelings*. Yes, you have paid good money to be told how to let your feelings out, and then perhaps ended up wallowing in them. But did your life change because of them? Probably not. Well, your life *will* change when you put yourself in the driver's seat and let your feelings and emotions take orders from your head and not your hurts.

A Spiritual Genius manages time so it is spent in productive ways and not in self-indulgence which generally gets you nowhere fast. This is the first step in becoming a Spiritual Genius.

CHAPTER FOUR

Yes, You Are Special and Unique, But Not *That* Special, So Get Over Yourself!

Aha! Here's the first contradiction in terms causing the mind to bend, the guts to swirl and the nerves to jangle. "What do you mean?," you ask. The Spiritual Genius says, "We are and yet we are not, at the same time. It is the perfect balance of the natural law of opposites contained within the same idea. In this Spiritual Truth, both Yin and Yan are needed to complete the whole. Think of it as 'life' or 'energy' where both positive and negative electrons are required to make an atom and create electrical energy."

The true meaning of the chapter title is that we are both the center of the universe and a small part of it at the very same time. At first glance we may only see the dialectical opposite, which gives us psychological whiplash. Upon deeper exploration, we find the Absolute Truth. Here is the place we fall softly into security.

There is One Thing "out there" and "in here," and it is nothing but energy. It was the first of its kind and the only of its kind. Some people have called it God. Others call it Cosmos, Universe, Energy, The Force, and so on. Whatever *you* want to call it, go ahead and name it, call it bubblegum, but get yourself into a quiet state where you really and truly know there is something that is Creation itself. It isn't someone or something that invented Creation, but it is the very presence of and essence of Creation itself. It is not *The* Creator, it is *CREATION*. Within that concept is the idea of Creation, plus the potential of Creation and the act of Creation, all rolled into One. "Three concepts in one!" So you've got this energetic compilation of "cosmic stuff" that we speak of as Creation; you have the Idea or Mind that organizes a concept around it; and then you have the actual "act" which translates all of this raw material into something outside of itself. Actually, it still *is* itself, but changes its external form while remaining what it is in its first essence.

If you're thinking this is nothing more than "rabble" (religious babble) then read it all again.

Heck, read Plato, he'll tell you the same darn thing. So will the *Bhagavad Gita*, but if you can't pronounce that, you surely shouldn't read it.

If this concept is still as frightening to you as an acid bubble bath, then do this:

> **Exercise**: Go to the ocean. Take a plastic container with you. Dip your container in the water and fill it up. Take that cup of ocean back home with you. Spend fifteen minutes trying to convince yourself this is not ocean. You see, because you have a container of sea water on your table does not change the fact that it is part of the whole ocean. It can never *not* be ocean, even if it is in your hand or in a container and you're standing on a porch in Missouri. That's exactly what we're talking about. You are the same as that container of ocean water. You are part of the big body of creative water even if you are not currently co-mingled with the rest of it in the big picture. You are and always will be part of the whole of Creation. It converts that phrase by Descartes, "I think, therefore I am" into *"I am, therefore I am."* — Spiritual Genius

From that premise of wholeness and cosmic unity we begin our next journey.

Following are some ideas on how you can experience this passage from the self into the whole. You can do any of these exercises in about fifteen minutes.

EXERCISES: Five Proven Ways to Connect to the One Great Power/ Cosmos/Creation/God/Energy and Experience it for Yourself.

(These are all experiential meditations. You will need to set aside some time to do these exercises. They are pleasant if you regularly *sit in stillness*; they are essential if you have not "connected" before.)

Exercise #1: Put on some quiet, easy listening or meditation music. Dim the lights. Set a timer for fifteen minutes. Relax completely. Take a few breaths, slowly inhaling and exhaling. Close your eyes. Really listen to the music. Hear the orches- trations. Hear the words, if there are any. Then "listen" more deeply to the music. Do you notice any "structure" or "pattern"? What can you hear "under" and "above" the piece? What is really going on? Can you "feel" any of the music? Can you feel the beat? Does it bring anything to mind? How do you feel when you listen? Go even further into the musical piece. What else can you sense? Use all of your senses to experience this moment. Is there a taste? A feeling? A texture? A smell? Identify the sounds. Does this music make you feel connected to people? A place? A thing? An animal? A memory? When you have explored all of these possibilities, or when the timer has sounded, open your eyes and recall your experiences. If you can, write them down so you can read them again later.

Exercise #2: Put on some soft music (calming, classical, meditation, soothing background). Turn the volume up to immerse yourself in the sound. Next, turn your TV channel to *Animal Planet* or *Discovery*. Tune in to a documentary that features animals in the wild. Turn the TV volume *off.* Allow the music on the stereo to complement the images on the TV. Notice that even without prior planning they fit together. Now, sit back. Take some deep breaths and breathe yourself into a relaxed state. Watch and listen. Pay attention to the movement of the animals. Listen to the music. See how the pattern and harmony of the two fall easily together. Do this for fifteen to twenty minutes. Just allow it all to unfold. Sense the great cosmic unity in this experiment. Experience how this random act of coupling produced harmony of sound and picture. Allow yourself some amazement and then accept what just happened as your connection to a Divine Guidance and a Universal Presence that exists beyond the here and now, and involves everyone and everything.

Exercise #3: Take a walk in a natural preserve, a botanical garden or a forest. You will look, touch and listen to the life present in this environment as you have never looked, touched or listened before. Allow yourself five minutes for each part of this exercise. Find a solitary place where you can have privacy. Get comfortable. Choose a piece of nature (stone, leaf, flower, plant) and observe it. *Really* look at it. Observe it so thoroughly that you could draw it from memory if you had to. When you think you've looked enough, continue looking for another two minutes and discover even more.

Next, find something that has a texture to it. Choose something you can hold or touch, such as tree bark. Close your eyes and feel this item with your hands. Then, rub it lightly over your leg, arm, cheek. Notice if anything changes. Press it hard. Touch it softly. See if touching it in several ways alters it in any way. Spend five minutes doing this.

Now open your listening capacity and hear the sounds around you. Pick one sound to concentrate on. When you have done that, hone in on it. Close your eyes. Allow nothing but that sound to be present for you. Stay with it for five minutes. Notice if it changes in any way. Notice everything about it. Are there patterns? Does it change in volume? If this sound were a color, what would it be? What does it remind you of?

When you have really listened for five minutes, pick up your touch object. Look at your original item of sight, feel your item of touch and listen to your sound. Allow them all to connect and notice how they are joined and how they are different. You have experienced each one as separate; now see what results when you put these sensory impressions together. What do you feel? Take a few moments to explore the sensations. Allow the sound to increase and decrease. Allow the colors to present themselves. Change the way you touch the item and look deeply into your first image. Play with the intensities as you would the volume knob on a radio. Bring them in and out of range. Notice how your perception changes and yet everything remains the same. After twenty minutes of this exercise, put your objects down, stand up and slowly reenter the world.

Exercise #4:   Allow yourself a time to meditate. Sit comfortably in a quiet space. No music, no outside interference. Just sit. Close your eyes. Pay attention to your breathing. Allow your breath to find its own rhythm. As your breath begins to slow, quietly repeat in your mind the words, *"I am."* Repeat this slowly and continuously for fifteen minutes. Allow thoughts to zip through your mind like passing cars. Do not dwell on any one thought. Let them float in and out. As the thoughts naturally slow down, begin to allow your breath to take you more deeply into relaxation.

When you feel as relaxed as you ever have been, allow the "I am" repetition to stop as you listen to what the small voice inside has to say. Just listen. Allow it to speak. Do not challenge it, contradict it, reason with it or negate it. Just listen as attentively and tenderly as you would to your best friend. Listen. When the voice has had a chance to speak its message, gradually allow yourself to hear the sounds in the room, and slowly bring yourself back to a fully conscious state. You should feel refreshed, centered and calm. Take a few moments to absorb this experience before returning to the activities of the world.

Exercise #5: Book a massage for yourself. Ask the masseuse not to talk to you during the massage. Ask that soft background music be played. Pick your favorite fragrance, or bring massage oil with an aroma that is relaxing and soothing. As you are being massaged, mentally follow the hands of the masseuse as they traverse your body. Travel with your mind to each area that is touched, lightly bringing oxygen into it. Relax and heighten your keen awareness of the touch.

Avoid the temptation to fall asleep. Use this time for conscious awareness of your body and how it feels. Sense tension being released as the hands move across your flesh. Experience the warmth. Focus on the process and stay with the movement of the hands. Connect. Then connect even more. Keep focusing until you reach a true sense of being at one with the hands, the motions and the sensations. Allow that unification to deepen for you until you feel no separation between your body and the masseuse's hands. When the massage is complete, retain that experience for the rest of the day. Whenever you come into contact with another person or object, recall that feeling of unity and connection. Let yourself have a visceral experience of wholeness and connection.

You must get yourself into a feeling-based experience of this oneness. It is a stepping stone to Spiritual Genius. Without this building block, you can't go any further. You will always feel separate, special or alone until you understand this Truth in your entire being. The deep feeling of unity with all creation gives you purpose; and with purpose, love, compassion and joy fall right into place.

CHAPTER FIVE

Never Let Your Mouth Write a Check Your "ASS" Can't Cash.

"What?" you say. The Spiritual Genius wants to get your attention! We are not talking about the donkey Jesus rode into town. We're talking about *your* very own "ASS," which in this instance stands for: "Active Spiritual Sense." This principle is clear and demands that you not put more on your plate than you can reasonably eat, and that you don't make promises you can't live up to, hence writing a check your assets can't cover.

First, we begin with ourselves. How many times have we made New Year's resolutions and then not kept one of them? Do you know that every time you *lie* to yourself, you prove that you don't *trust* yourself? That's right. When you say you're going to be somewhere to meet somebody and you don't show up, what happens? How does that *somebody* feel? They probably think you're a flake, that you are irresponsible, and they most likely feel very pissed off that you had the bad manners to keep them waiting and stand them up. Right? Ask yourself this: if this had been an appointment to receive a shopping bag full of hundred-dollar bills, would you have been late or not shown up? If this were an interview for the job you've always dreamed of, would you have been late? If this were a big dinner and you were the guest of honor, would you have just not arrived? Of course not. (If you answered "yes" to any of those questions, please call some kind of head doctor and check yourself into the closest demented thinking center.) Presumably, if you're not reaching for the phonebook, you answered "no." So, let's continue.

When we tell little lies to ourselves we do tremendous damage to our souls. We end up subconsciously not believing anything we think or say is true. How could we? If we have a friend who is a chronic liar, do we trust this person? When we continually make promises to ourselves that we repeatedly break, we are actually fighting the feelings of goodness down deep inside and we end up not being able to distinguish our own truth from a lie. Then we go out into the world and tell more, and more and more lies. Pretty soon, we're a mess of little white lies. It begins small, becomes a habit, and then it gets out of hand leaving us feeling icky. So, we reach for the bottle or the pill, we over-work ourselves at the gym, we tear around trying to get the spiritual equivalent of napalm off our chests when all we really need to do is start telling the truth again. To *ourselves*.

Speak the truth to yourself. If you want to accomplish something, take a realistic look at yourself. At thirty-eight years old you're not going to begin training for the Olympic gold medal in skating, but you can do other things. If you want to avoid disappointing yourself and telling yourself you are "dumb," an "idiot" or a "moron," then offer yourself achievable goals.

The Spiritual Genius borrows from corpo-rate America for this lesson. There is a catch phrase in senior management groups that uses an acronym for goals and achievement. They call it "*SMART*" which stands for: *Specific, Measurable, Achievable, Results, Timing.*

Specific means you need to identify all of the parts. You don't just say, "Gimme a sandwich," you say, "I'd like a ham and swiss cheese sand-wich on a sourdough roll with Dijon mustard." Be very specific about what you want to achieve, and make note of all the steps that go with it. For example, grocery shopping is an eight-part activity. You first have to make a list, then you drive to the market. Next you put the items in your basket. Then you pay for them. After that you put them in your car, take them home, bring them inside and put them away. Bet you never thought of grocery shopping as having eight parts, did you? Well, now you have to look at everything in terms of its components.

Measurable means you have to create a standard of some sort by which to measure your progress toward the goal. Usually it can be reduced to gain or loss which needs to be charted in some fashion. Your psyche needs to be able to "see" in a linear fashion the progress of the activity. This is also the way we actively motivate ourselves to go on toward completion. Don't deny your subconscious the thrill of measurement.

Attainable is your sanity check clause. Can this goal actually and realistically be accomplished? Just because you want to attain /achieve something doesn't necessarily mean it can be attained. (A seventy-five-year-old man is probably not going to attain a gold medal in the Olympic Triathlon no matter how long or hard he exercises, but he could enter in the Senior Olympics and probably win.)

Make sure you don't kid yourself with this step. This isn't your license to avoid attempting something because of doubt, fear, lack of faith or laziness. You simply need to be honest with yourself about whether your goal is realistic and actually attainable.

Results mean outcome. Ask youself: What is gained by this goal? What changes in my life because this goal is accomplished? What improves? You can break this down into a personal framework or into global considerations. You must clearly state what you personally have to gain when the goal is achieved, and/or what everyone else gains if you achieve it. It is usually wise to have both personal and global components in your plan. You will find that support is more forthcoming when a collective gain is entwined with the end goal.

Timing is as critical as all of the above elements. You don't plant tomatoes in January in an outside garden if you live in Maine. You may however, plant them in January if you live in Central America. You must take the time to think your goal through and make informed decisions. Admittedly, this is fairly obvious, but "timing" is also critical in the more elusive areas as well.

If Starbucks is planning to open up a new store on a particular corner in three months, it probably isn't a good idea to open your own coffee shop next door. They have loads more marketing and advertising and a brand-name. Your dream may be to have a coffee bar of your own, but don't make your success dependant on "luck" instead of careful planning. Don't rush! You really must ask the right questions and do the detail work if you want to be successful.

The Spiritual Genius says, "You have all the creative energy necessary to achieve your goals/dreams/wishes/hopes." Help yourself by using every brain cell and every planning tool to make the journey as *SMART* as you can. You will be ever more willing to accept the unplanned events that life offers you if your basic foundation is solid. If it is firm it can withstand a few jolts. There is a reason skyscrapers are now built on wheels. They reach for the sky but have a flexible base so they can roll with the punches of nature.

The key point of *SMART* is to take more than just a single moment to organize your thinking before you shoot your wad. Keep this in mind: *SMART* advice is only for the things you can control in your life—those things that you consciously set yourself up to do.

Let's take a common example to explain the process: weight loss. It is not impossible for a 300-pound woman to lose weight even though she works for Krispy Kreme. It has all to do with *SMART* planning. What she has to do is figure out a simple ratio: calories in versus energy out—how many calories can she put in her body in direct relation to how many calories she burns off. It's *that* simple.

She can specify her desired weight loss goal quite easily. She can take a look at any calorie counter and then calculate what she is putting into her body and break it down by item. Cup of coffee, piece of toast, three jelly donuts. Add those up and bingo, you have a breakfast total (800). Next, move on to lunch: a Big Mac, fries and a Coke (900). Afternoon snack: chocolate éclair (200). Add those to dinner: a frozen Hungry Man dinner and a bowl of ice cream (1,000). Got it? Now, adding breakfast, lunch and dinner together, you come up with about 3000 calories. If she burns off 2,000 calories a day working an eight-hour shift, she's storing 1000 extra calories a day somewhere.

Not too hard to figure out. Just reduce the amount of calories ingested to fit with the calories burned off and you *maintain* your weight. Reduce the intake to the output and you *lose* weight. Add exercise to increase the output and you lose *more* weight and much faster. No other diet system in the world is more effective than measuring and controlling intake versus output.

Our 300-pound woman's challenge becomes not the mathematics but the *choices* she makes now that she has the info. Will she or won't she cut down on the calories she puts in her body to be more balanced with the energy she exerts? It could work as long as she doesn't lie to herself and tell herself: a) it's genetic, I can't lose the weight; b) I've always failed, diets don't work for me; c) it's too hard/it's too hot/I have too many kids/ my feet hurt/I'm happy this way/my mother needs me/my husband doesn't complain/my sister picked on me as a kid/my classmates called me "pork-butt" in fifth grade but I don't care. If she lies to herself, it won't work. She'll write a check her "ASS" can't cash, because she's made it impossible to believe the words she says, thereby thwarting all actions taken. It's like pouring a gallon of water into a bucket riddled with holes and then blaming the bucket for leaking. However, if she's more realistic, maps out a plan and gives herself the *SMART* system, she'll succeed. She will be able to see all the components clearly, get beyond the feelings and emotions surrounding the subject that may be restricting her progress, and tackle the goal one step at a time.

When writing a check with your mouth, be sure you ask your "ASS" if it can make the payment. Ask the right questions, tell the truth and set up a system of communication between your mouth and your "ASS" that always tells the truth and follows through. If your "ASS" doesn't trust your mouth, it won't cooperate. It won't cash the check. Do not disappoint yourself with lies and false promises or you'll be stuck with a mess of bounced checks.

You know how wild the bank becomes when you overdraw your account? Ever tried to have a conversation with a teller when your account is overdrawn? You feebly attempt to make excuses about why that happened and promise to refill that account next week. Remember the expression on his/her face? Now you know how your soul feels when you make excuses and tell fibs to it. Picture that teller's face the next time you tell yourself a white lie. The Spiritual Genius says, "Nobody but you can hang your own 'ASS' out to dry."

Use the following chart whenever you start out to achieve a goal.

The SMART System

Specific: Write a clear statement of what you want to achieve and list all the components in the process.	
Measurable: Construct an accounting system with steps that need to be met.	
Attainable: Is your goal realistic? List all the pros and cons.	
Results: What is the outcome/benefit for you plus the larger group?	
Timing: List the time frame in which this goal needs to be accomplished.	

CHAPTER SIX

In the Beginning Was the Word.

Do you remember that phrase from Sunday school or shul? Even if you're not a western Christian or Jew, you would have had to be living in a bat cave not to have heard that phrase with which St. John begins his Gospel in the New Testament.

Consider this quote from GeoCities: "Certainly in Hebrew thought 'the Word' (*debar*) is significant. 'By the word of the Lord were the Heavens made, and all their hosts by the breath of His mouth' (Old Testament, Psalm 33.6). This links with Genesis 1 where 'God said' and it was done. Thus the term signifies the powerful, creative Word of God, (that this Word is in the Mind of God, John 1.3 makes clear), and the Word is the One who carries out the work of creation."

The Spiritual Genius says, "Don't be fooled by the literal idea of the word 'word.'" What we are really talking about is thought, *spoken* thought from the Universal Mind. That which begins as an idea in the mind and then makes its way through the pathways of the brain and out through the mouth into the world as we know it. It is the Word. It is Creation. The key point to remember is: You always have the last "word," no matter what. You control what you think. "That's preposterous," you say, "How in the holy heck do I control what my mind thinks?" Ha hah! Read on, because that's a key point of this book, and you'll see how you do, in fact, control everything you think and feel. Stay with me!

There are many kinds of *words* spoken in our society. Imagine what might have been the first word ever spoken. Who "said" what to whom? And more importantly, what was the first *reaction*? We use words to communicate something. If we lived alone in a cave on the hill, we wouldn't need to speak. Who would be there to hear us? Words are tools used for the sole purpose of being understood.

Humans have a primal need to be understood. Cats meow, dogs bark and chicks peep. That's how they seek and get attention. For dependent animals a noise usually means "provide something for me—food/shelter/ warmth—or do something to me— pet/scratch/comb/help." The benefits reaped for both involved in those communications is the experience of affection and love.

As babies we use sounds to communicate our needs: *waaaaaaaaah,* usually means "I'm hungry, I'm tired, I hurt, I'm uncomfortable," etc. We need another human with a more sophisticated use of their limbs to *do* some-thing for us, to assist our daily living experi-ence, or we die. To avoid fatality we make our *waaaaaaaaah* as loud as it can be.

As maturing humans we learn to stop using *waaaaaaaaah* to communicate our needs and we employ words as our tools to get them met. As our words increase, so does our ability to think of more things to communicate. We don't just want a dress, we want a *red* dress. We don't just want nourishment, we want a *rare steak.* Maturity gives us adjectives that, in turn, allow our lives layers of meaning. This achievement leads us directly to the concept of "discernment." Sorting out *what* we want and then using the correct words to accom-plish that end are the real skills.

If we use words that are weak, we will get weak things. If we use words that have power, we will get powerful things. Like attracts like.

We speak on two levels. There is the "inner dialog" we have with ourselves. And there is our outer dialog, those words we speak that say more about us than we know. Actions may speak louder than words, but let's use Eliza Doolittle (or for the purists, *Pygmalion*) as our example.

Eliza was a poor little waif-like flower girl in the streets of London. To win a bet, Professor Henry Higgins picked her up, took her home and cleaned up both her body (by bath) and her language (by repetition). He grilled her with lesson after lesson until she pronounced words correctly. He wanted round, warm sounds which emanated from deep inside her diaphragm and not those squeaky, raspy sounds which came out her nose. He forced her to walk with books piled high on her head to straighten her posture. He taught her manners, and the art of conversation, and filled her head with stories and ideas. One action led to another until he had her speaking, breathing and walking with ease and grace. From her lips came words that sounded elegant and brought her a new confidence.

She was in her glory and the happiest she'd ever been in her life when she was applauded, accepted and admired "at the ball." She felt the power of her words because they were *effective.* She watched people respond to her as they had never responded before. She curtsied; they bowed. She extended her hand and high-ranking gentlemen kissed her glove! She continued to follow this formula, and the more it worked, the stronger she got.

You can do the same thing. If you are not getting what you want and achieving the results you want *(SMART)* then think of yourself as the little flower person in the streets of London and take yourself home, give yourself a warm bath and then get the heck on with the task of retraining yourself and making yourself word-fit for the ball.

To begin, what do you think about yourself and how do you express it? Do you find that you are always calling yourself names, (like when you do something less than perfectly)? When the hammer hits your thumb instead of the nail, when that glass of orange juice slips and falls to the floor, breaking your favorite glass, what are your first "words?" If calling yourself names is a habit, then please select a couple of your most recent "name callings" from the list below. Trade them out for the opposite word on the next list.

Dummy	Smarty
Moron	Macaroon
Idiot	Idol
Stupid	Clever
Asshole	Comic
Jerk	Jester
Fool	Genius
Turkey	Swan

If you are rolling your eyes and about ready (again) to toss this book out of an open window, hang on. You actually *may like* where this goes. Just take another deep breath and read through this chapter before you toss. C'mon! You can play along for a little longer.

Let's say you're on the freeway and some driver cuts you off, forcing you to swerve and brake so as not to hit him. What's the first "word" that comes to mind? Is it "sweetie?" The Spiritual Genius says, "Change your mind first, and the words will follow. If you want to yell, "moron" think instead, "macaroon." If you *think* about something sweet or more pleasing, you'll feel more pleasant, and your whole day will go better." "Barf!

Now I'm really gonna hurl! That's ridiculous," you say, "not to mention stupid. If I want to call somebody a jerk I have the right, especially when he did *that* to me." Right? Wrong! Words are serious business.

Power words are those that communicate uplifting and invigorating emotions to ourselves and to others. They create powerful and instantaneous change. If you don't believe me, then try them for yourself.

Use the power of choice and the tool of substitution to create a kinder and gentler environment for yourself. If you are still dubious, then be willing to try the experiment for twenty four hours. See what develops as a result. Come on! You can do it!

(See the following page for a list of power words.)

These are the power words of life:

Love	Happy	Wealth	Prosperity
Choice	Abundance	Good	Thank you
Please	Forgiveness	Happiness	Freely
Flow	Peace	Generosity	Harmonious
Beautiful	Agree	Joyful	Appreciate
Magnificent	Growth	Strength	Worthy
Illumination	Music	Butterfly	Cleansing
Spontaneous	Lightness	Play	Clarity
Whole	Merge	Align	Renew(al)
Synchronicity	Grateful	Tolerance	Trust
Acknowledge	Wisdom	Experience	Truth
Understanding	Loyalty	Patient	Integrity
Reflect	Courage	Honesty	Sharing
Reverence	Respect	Cheerful	Knowledge
Prayer	Empower	Enjoy	Alive
Willing	Confident	Breathe	Fun
Laugh(ing)	Love	Risk	Enhance
Life	Assimilation	Blessing	Creative

The very next time you want to say something to express a need, an emotion or a desire, look over this list. Include one or two of these words and your communication will be more effective. Copy the "power word" page; take it with you. See what happens. Take any old sentence you were about to use, and exchange words from the list for a few of the negative or inflammatory words. Experiment. It's easy and just takes a little practice. Play with it for a couple of days and see what results.

So back to the "macaroon" example for a moment. This is just another way to look at the power of your words. This practice *will* give a new depth and help you clarify your intentions as expressed through your words. You will begin to *feel* a shift moments after you begin.

The process of substituting "macaroon" for "moron" came to me as a result of traffic in a major city, a decision to stay in the metropolis and not move to the country, plus the realization nothing was going to change, no matter what I said in my car. I could either change my thinking and be happier in the moment, or continue to be riled at yet another driver as if he were the reason for the wait/delay/problem/frustration, and ultimately have a heart attack one day from excess rage. Just as a growing baby changes its sound from *waaaaaaaaah* to "momma" I decided to experiment with new languaging and see if it would affect my interior climate.

In such situations, the first thought that would always come to my mind was "Moron." With only a subtle shift it became "maroon," as if softening the color/feeling of "red" to a muted shade. Next came "macaroon" because that suggests even greater enjoyment. Hence, my words in traffic are now, "Thank you macaroon," or "Bless you, you creative spirit," or "That was really clever, you genius." Before you hiss and boo like a cat about to be plunged into water, *try it*! Be open! It won't kill you!

Once you master the word exchange (and tickle yourself with the absolutely delightful magic of the transformation), just wait until someone is riding in the car with you and they hear "the new you." You have a ton of joy-filled moments in store. Now, let's move from words into phrases.

By the time we've reached the age of ten, we are well aware that life doesn't come with a plan. At fifteen we know people don't come with a manual, and at twenty we learn relationships don't come with guarantees.

So what is reliable? The Internet? Certainly not the weather! The correct answer is: *your thinking and speaking.*

You can change the way you think about your life and everybody else's. The primary key is changing what you say and how you say it. If you are willing to commit a few key phrases to memory, you can immediately transform your life and the lives around you. Your life is guaranteed to shift, and isn't that why you bought this book in the first place? We'll get into the heavier subject of how you think in a later chapter. For now, just take a cursory look at the following phrases and be willing to consider what would happen if you used *them* instead of your usual fare. Remember, this book is a series of shortcuts. Master them and you will live fulfilled.

Three Sets of Four Transformational Words

1. I'll be right there.

How many times have you wished you could have heard that? From your parents? From your siblings? From your teacher? Best friend? Lover? It doesn't matter if you are hurting from a physical wound or an emotional razor blade, just hearing those four little words makes all the difference to you in that moment. Say them to others, often. And then *show up*.

2. You may be right.

Thousands of marriage counselors would have vacant offices if more people in relationships would use these words. This phrase is not just for couples, but co-workers, teachers, students, politicians, wrestlers, bankers, grocery store clerks and everyone else as well. If we used this phrase and heard it back, the tsunami of conflict could be reduced to a mere ripple. Think for a moment of the words of The Terminator. If he had said, "You may be right," instead of "I'll be back," that phrase could just as easily have led to a sequel. It may have been a fuller story with a broader plot.

3. Listen to your heart.

How many of us wish we could have heard these words from our parents? Instead, they may have said, "You'll do it my way or the highway," or, "That won't work. Go get a real job," or "Do what you're told." Some of us did have parents who encouraged us to follow our hearts; many of us wished we had. We may even have "adopted" someone else's parent for the comfort we craved when we didn't have it at home. Doesn't it feel great when someone trusts you, or says to you, "Go ahead, follow your heart?" Don't we all want to be somebody's hero? Isn't that why many of us have children? We all want to be admired.

If you would be willing to adopt those *Three Sets of Four Transformational Words* as regular phrases in your everyday life, you will become a safe person for others to be around and become the parent we all wished we'd had. Spiritual Geniuses beget Spiritual Geniuses. You can begin today.

CHAPTER SEVEN

When All You Have Is a Hammer, Everything Looks Like a Nail.

What's in your tool chest? Wouldn't you want to choose an assortment of tools for yourself and not just limit yourself to one? Are you a bundle of "have to's" and "must do's" rather than "choose to's" and "wanna do's"? There is an entire business network in Europe linked to the key word "wannado." It deals with travel, leisure and fun things to do. The Spiritual Genius says, "Turn your life into a wanna do by increasing the variety of tools in your tool chest." You may wonder "what does a hammer have to do with vacation plans?" Or maybe you are thinking, "Why couldn't I have bought the book by Wayne Dyer or Deepak Chopra, instead of this one?" Well you could have, but reading this book and following its guidance will get you on the wanna do life path faster. Spiritual Genius is dedicated to short-cuts and knowing it all, fast.

Remember the person back in the early '90s who thought it was "cute" not to be able to program their VCR but who is now confronted with Tivo, DSL, and programmable water piks? Not being able to program a VCR these days requires remedial summer school for kindergartners! Programming skills are tantamount to survival in our techno-laden society. Just resetting digital timers and clocks after a power outage is a four-hour task. The point is, you have to leave the confines of your mental township in order to expand the working latitude of your mind. You must have more tools if you are to survive, progress and create a standard of living above that of a crustacean. The alternative is to remain dependent on outdated technology and live in the techno cave age.

Some people are classic hammers. The psychological profession calls them narcissists, and they see the world and people in it only as something or someone to benefit them. Narcissists view people and opportunities as nails. They wouldn't be nearly as pathological if they viewed the world as a hammer, wrench and saw. They would have other perspectives and more options. They would also widen the spectrum of their own experience.

It is impossible to build an entire house with just a hammer and a nail. You have to use some screwdrivers and other tools along the way. So how do you begin? For starters, you go shopping. The Spiritual Genius says, "Take yourself to the 'hardware store of life' and look up and down the aisles. See what's available to you." Notice there are *many* different types of tools and many different types of applications for each tool. Experiment. Select a new tool and try it out. Suggestion: start simple; don't get the entire set of power tools until you know the basics of a few key tools and understand electricity.

Then, sign up for some instruction. Don't just go out and purchase a garage full of supplies and then sit in your driveway wondering what the heck to do with them. Decide first what you want to build, then get the help/advice /instructions that will take you step by step through the process. You wouldn't buy all the scuba gear and suit up if you didn't intend to eventually go in the water would you? And then you wouldn't actually dive in without some instruction unless you had a built-in death wish!

When you select your life tools, make sure they are always top quality. Don't go for the beaten up, used kind. Acquire the best tools you can afford and take care of them. Don't leave your tools out in the rain. The wooden handles will rot, the metal will rust, and they will ultimately fall apart on you when you least expect it, usually in the middle of a project. To avoid calamity, care for your tools. Keep them clean and oil them once in a while. They will last longer and serve you better. "But I don't like hardware stores," you complain. Oh, calm down. Just go along with the metaphor for a moment.

In life, we need the best tools we can get our hands on to face the competition in a marketplace that is looking for qualified people who possess honed skills, toned emotional muscles and good phone manners. As a Spiritual Genius you have to make *all* the parts of life work for you. That means you must support yourself through gainful means; create a life of mutual and reciprocal support around you, your work and your family; sustain and nurture relationships that are healthy and bear fruit; live as an example of positive principles and give back generously to the areas of life that sustain, nurture and inspire you. As a Spiritual Genius you do not retire to the mountains, live off nuts and berries and cloister yourself from all of Spirit's fine world. You participate fully in that life into which you have incarnated.

In order to accomplish all of that, you as a Spiritual Genius need a full set of tools that you can utilize and rely upon as you build your life. You may find you need to purge old thinking, old patterns of anger, addiction, blame, projection, narcissism, weight, education, language, attitude, or other emotional or physical cages you have kept yourself in. The ideas in this book provide you with the tools and exercises you can use to strengthen your character and deepen your Spiritual Roots.

If you are not getting what you want in life, take a good, clear, hard look at what might be in your way. There is a magazine advertisement from the 1990s that says: "It's not what you're eating that matters, it's what's eating you." True. Turn your melodrama into a mellow drama. Get the help and the tools you need to succeed, and then get out of your own way and watch what happens. When you own a plethora of tools, you'll be able to use a hammer when you see a nail, use a saw when you want to cut through something, use a wrench when you want to tighten a nut and use a screwdriver when you want to secure a screw. Each has its own application and purpose. You'll know that automatically and choose the proper tool for the job. Become a master carpenter and not just an inept apprentice. You'll be able to build a skyscraper if that's what you choose to do with your well-stocked tool chest. Just like the pros. And wouldn't you really rather be a pro than a con? (The Spiritual Genius probably should apologize profusely for that pun!—but I don't.) Still confused about what tools you need? Read on! There's more to learn.

CHAPTER EIGHT

Trust In God and Tie Your Camel.

"Trust in God, *but* tie your camel" is the first version of this slogan I ever read. So what happened to the "but"? It went out with the old way of thinking! It's all in a word, you know. When adjusting your thinking, you also have to adjust your language. If you say to someone "I really like you, but...," you put them on the defensive. The other person instantly *feels* a boom of some sort is about to be lowered onto their head. However, if you say "I really like you, and..." the listener remains attentive because you have said something positive, and they are expecting you will add something equally nice to the sentence. When you choose to use "and" instead of "but," you are also more likely to say something kinder and more productive.

First way: *"I really like you, but you make it hard for me to work when you play that rap music at your desk."*

Improved way: *"I really like you, and I would appreciate it if we could find a compromise for the volume of your music as I find I am distracted by it."*

The first sentence sounds like a benign attack and makes the other person wrong for playing their choice of music. The second sentence takes them off the hook and places the discomfort on you, not them. As a result, they are 100 times more apt to cooperate with you. Wouldn't you? "Yeah, but he/she makes me mad. Who do they think they are, anyway, playing *that* music when I'm trying to work?" Well, most likely they *aren't* thinking and if they *are* thinking, they are thinking about themselves. Given you are approaching a potentially emotionally-charged situation anyway, why not go into it stepping as lightly as possible? It's subtle, and we are looking for *results*, not deciding who's right.

"Trust in God, *and* tie your camel" is about *results.* It has a twofold meaning. The first fold illustrates the difference "and" rather than "but" can make in your life. Replacing "and" for "but" can make peace where guns are drawn and plant flowers where once there were barren rocks. The second fold clarifies taking care of yourself and those things you care about. If you go to all the trouble of buying a camel and riding him someplace, don't leave him loose so he can wander off by himself, be removed by a well-intentioned helper or worse, stolen by an out-and-out thief. Tie your camel! For those of you who are about to call Brinks Security and have your house locked up like Fort Knox, relax. We're speaking in metaphor.

Many of us work hard to acquire something and then we don't do what's necessary to secure it. We tell too many people about our idea and it is put into use without our name being attached. Or, perhaps we buy something new and wonderful then loan it out to someone else who does not have the same value system and it is returned to us battered and broken. What were we thinking? "But I trusted them!" you moan. Well, perhaps you shouldn't have. Trust God; God doesn't need your ideas or your stuff. But be discerning about the people in whom you put your trust (and your property). It's like the old Bible phrase, "Don't cast your pearls among swine."

No one is going to appear out of the mist and save you from yourself. Make *sound* judgments and don't allow yourself to be a pushover or trust that anyone else is going to look out for you as well or better than you look out for yourself. There is no Prince Charming and there is no Magic Genie. There is only a Spiritual Genius who tells you to monitor and protect that which you consider to be your very own personal talents, possessions or assets.

If you lose them by way of your own neglect or default, how will you replace them? Worse, how much time will you waste moaning about the loss, grieving over its absence and then blaming yourself for being a macaroon? (Get out your timer!) Or worse yet, will you blame someone else for being careless, thoughtless or selfish when you knew that's who they were all along and you still lent it to them? Is it *really* their fault for being who they are, or is it *yours* for expecting them to behave beyond a capacity they possess? Learn the difference. You won't have to worry about the spilled milk if you hang firmly onto the glass in the first place. The only time you ought to untie your camel is when you want to move on to another place. Then mount that dromedary and head out full-tilt boogie.

Here are some phrases to help you avoid getting into a trap and feeling pressured to comply. Say the sentence and then *shut up*. Resist the temptation to explain further.

"I would love to loan you my car, but I will be needing it for my own use. Let me help you figure out another way to get yourself to _____."

"You know I would love to be there/do that; unfortunately I am otherwise committed."

"At another time I may be willing to _____. At this moment I just simply can't."

"I have some other plans for (my camera, my new dress/my _____.) Perhaps another time."

"With advance notice, I may have been able to _____. That's not the case right now."

"Thank you so much for your thoughtful concern. I'll be just fine. Perhaps another time I can take you up on your offer."

"Let me give that some thought and get back to you." (Here's where you "buy some time" to think it over and figure out something else clever to say.)

Use these examples to make a complete list of your own "phrases for all occasions" and have them always handy so you can pull them out when needed (or, better yet, commit them to memory). Being prepared for the unexpected (and unwanted) you will mentally tie your camel and not squander your resources, all the while trusting in God.

CHAPTER NINE

"Good Grief," said Charlie Brown, and Other Oxymacaroons.

In the full panoply of life there are always two sides to every seesaw. The Spiritual Genius says, *"One day you're the pigeon, and the next day you're the statue."* And how do we know which one we'll be when we get up in the morning? We don't! The Spiritual Genius says, "Plan to wake up as the pigeon, but take along some Handi Wipes just in case you become the statue."

Every day we set out on our course. More than likely we have an idea of how it will be. We have prepared our tools, we have filled our minds with powerful possibilities and we are open to the carnival of life. Then, "splat," we are covered with the unexpected and we cry out at the top of our spiritual lungs, "Aw, Shift!" (They say "Shift happens!" And it does!) Suddenly, our course is altered by another person, an incident, an accident, an invasion. We are no longer in the proverbial driver's seat. We have been felled by an external circumstance. Our plans are upended. We have been disrupted by a person, place or thing and we feel like the statue. What do we do now?

The first thing to do is assess the damage. How severe was this blow to us (on a scale of one to ten)? Are we actually harmed, or merely embarrassed? Are we injured, or just annoyed? Calculate the *real* not the *apparent* damage. We have to separate how we *feel* from how it truly is or appears to be.

Remember back when you were in grade school and the person you had a crush on took someone else to the dance? (Feel free to fill in the blanks here with what your experience was.) In that moment, you felt like you could never face another day. You felt betrayed, humiliated, dumped, trashed, lonely, frustrated and probably a bit angry and jealous. A year later or ten years later, did you still feel the same way? Were you able to laugh about it? Are you able to laugh about it now? Feelings don't last; memories do. You can absolutely choose how you remember this moment by how you deal with it on a feeling level in the present. Assess the actual damage, and then move into damage control and rapid repair.

Are you twitching? I can sense it. "This is no time for mercy! I caught _____ in _____ with _____! How the heck am I supposed to get over that?" The Spiritual Genius says, "I never said it was easy. When you are living a conscious life at a highly conscious level, you simply take the time to heal the wound; no more, no less."

The minute you experience being the statue, bring out a "Handi Wipe" and become the pigeon again. "Handi Wipes" should always be in your tool chest. They wipe away the debris. Keep an ample supply on hand. Here are some "Handi Wipes" to help you survive the "statue" days.

Handi Wipes

1. Create a file for yourself in which you save all the nice things anyone ever says to you, sends you or gives you. You need two types of files: One is a physical file folder to keep thank you notes, Xerox copies of sayings, poems and inspiration, along with cherished cards which have special words written on them. (If you're really anal, organize a binder with divided

sections and "pockets" to hold things.) You can also keep a hard disk copy of inspirational sayings or stories from the Internet and E-mail. When you hit a pothole in the road of life and you're feeling washed out and worthless, pull out these files and force yourself to read some of them. You will regain a sense of how others really see you so that you can imbibe the message and pull yourself up.

2. Music is key. Know the songs that lift your spirits. Make a list if you think you'll forget and keep it in your palm pilot or planner. Then play the songs for yourself. Warning: Country & Western Music is a trap. It's always about somebody doing somebody wrong. Don't play those songs unless there is a message to lift you up (rather than giving you permission to wallow and howl).

3. Humor! This is not a suggestion to trivialize or deny what has just occurred. The key word here is "perspective." What will you think and feel about this situation in five years? Try to leap ahead into that future time frame and look back. If you can gain perspective, you may be able to make mental notes that will, in time,

make you laugh. If you are able to disassociate with the pain of the moment and go *way* into the future, you will gain perspective and faster healing. The time *will* come when you do look back and, if you are to grow and mature at all, this will be one of those treasured moments that builds your character and leads you forth into a greater day.

4. Allow yourself a certain amount of time to heal. Check the end of Chapter Three to see if any of your situations appear on the list. They may. If so, pick a time you are willing to be "off the charts" and set that time aside to grieve, cry and have your emotions. Create a ritual around the grief if you need to. See below for more ideas if you need additional assistance.

Creative Ways to Release, Grieve and Express Emotion So You Can Heal

Matters of the heart: If you feel you have been hurt, betrayed or wronged, then get out a pen and paper. You're going to sit down and write three letters.

1. The first letter begins, *Dear* _____ (the name of the person who wronged you). State what was done, how you feel

about it and what you'd like the person to do to make it up.

2. The second letter begins, *Dear _____* (the name of a person in your life that you wronged). State what you did, state how you think the person feels about it, or how you would feel if it were done to you, and then write how you would like to make it up to them.

3. The third letter begins, *Dear _____* (write your own name). Write how you feel in this very moment. Write down what it would take to change your feelings. Then give it to yourself as if you are your very own angel. Forgive yourself if you need to for anything that needs to be repaired, restored or reinstated. Put this letter in an envelope, and address it to yourself.

Mail all three letters. By the time you receive the letter you wrote to yourself, you will have experienced a healing.

Loss of a loved one: If you have lost a parent, child, spouse, friend or close relative, this can leave you with a hole in your life. The place this person filled can be either huge or small depending on your relationship to them and your dependency. You grieve to the same degree that you have loved. You will want to alternate between feeling the loss for yourself and doing what needs to be done.

The first thing you want to do is honor what they gave you. You can do this by creating a special place in your home for them. In this place you can arrange photos, keepsakes and mementos of their presence in your life. Speak to those items about your feelings.

Tell these items how much you loved the person who left you and how much they are missed. Make the talk about the person, not you. You are here. You will heal. They have journeyed on. Tell them what they gave you. Write those gifts down. Place that paper in this special area. If you were able to communicate this to them while they were alive, great. If not, do it now. Love has no sense of time. Say all the things you wanted to say and say them over and over.

When you have done that about ten times, sit quietly and think about what you gave them. What would they say to you if they were in your position? Make a list of the gifts you gave them and place them in this special area. Set aside ten minutes a day for the first month to do this process. Recall (or read) the gifts they gave and then recall (or read) the gifts you gave to them.

By the end of thirty days you will begin to feel complete with this process. Be sure to do it every day. If you can do it at the same time every day, your heart will rest because it will come to depend on this special time with the departed one. You may choose to repeat this process for a little longer.

After ninety days, stop the process. Reduce the time to five minutes a day if you still want the connection, and replace the rituals with stories you remember. Say them aloud if you can, and recall as much detail as you can. Try to find a new story for each day. Do this until you literally run out of stories.

One day, within a year, you will restructure this special place so it appropriately matches your newly healed state and signifies your life as it is in the present. Keeping fresh flowers in this special place is one way to always honor the memory and the gifts of the person who left you.

Adopt a puppy or a kitty. Put your love into a new life as soon as you can and name it after your/the loss.

Loss of job:

If you have been fired from a job you have *two* tasks.

1. Get out a piece of paper and make four columns. List in the first column all the things you liked/enjoyed about the job. In the second column list all the things you did *not* like/enjoy about the job. In the third column list all the things you could have changed about the job (not *would* have, *could* have). Now in the fourth column rate your frustration with each item (that you could or could not have changed) on a scale of 1 to 10, (10 being the highest). Add up the score.

   If you have over 50, you should write a thank you note to the person who fired you and let them know how grateful you are for their courage in allowing you to be free to search for employment that better utilizes your talents. Avoid sarcasm. Come from the place of sincere gratitude for this freedom to find something even better for yourself.

   If your score is 30 to 50 then you need to re-evaluate your participation in this work situation. Are there areas where you could have improved as an employee?

Was there a situation you could have improved by handling it more skillfully? Take a good look at your performance and be honest about what you may have done to co-create this parting of the ways.

If your score is under 30 then maybe you should go back there and figure out a way to apologize and get your job back. Perhaps you should have been grateful earlier; it's never too late to begin again. Order a full serving of Humble Pie, eat the whole thing and then start over.

2. Go out and purchase yourself two cards: One should be a "sympathy" card for your loss and the other should be a "congratulations" card for your gain. Write the appropriate words to yourself on each one. Address and mail the sympathy card to yourself, first. A day later, mail the congratulations card. See, don't you feel better already?

CHAPTER TEN

Forbidden Fruits Make Mighty Nice Jams.

When was the last time you felt a little naughty? Better yet, answer this: What exactly qualifies as *naughty* for you? Is it a thrill, a secret, something you "get away" with? Do you enjoy watching something, being watched, sneaking, peeking, touching, tasting? The synonyms for the word "naughty" range from "impish and frolicsome" to "unmanageable and corrupt." Where does your personal definition of naughty fit in?

"Naughty" often flies co-pilot in the next seat to "forbidden." Do you allow anything naughty in your life? Do you have a release valve for the impish, scampish little rogue inside yourself? Do you walk a line with those urges? Are you able to keep them within the law? You might be thinking, "What does any of this have to do with becoming a Spiritual Genius?" The answer is: *everything*! If you don't know what your forbidden fruits are, how are you possibly going to make a nice jam? If you don't recognize them and give them a forum, they will come out eventually in ways you may not be thrilled with, possibly causing your (or someone else's) blood pressure to rise. If you try to deny this streak or tendency in yourself, you'll end up with a case of repression that makes leprosy look like a slight skin rash.

Let's get out our Bibles once again and go back to the parable of Adam and Eve. Remember the apple and the snake? Who tempted whom, with what and why? If Eve had only picked the fruit and made a nice tidy batch of jam, she and Adam might still be back there as the reigning King and Queen of Paradise. I'm not talking about a luxury hotel in Las Vegas, I mean the real thing, *Nirvana.* They might very well have made the jam, bottled it and asked permission to spread it on hot cross buns. Instead, Eve gave in to her immediate craving and took a giant bite right out of that crunchy, yummy apple and then she and Adam got "Hasta la vista, Baby" read to their proverbial buns. *"Sayonara Paradise!"* and the gates slammed shut, forever.

The general consensus among Spiritual Geniuses is that the apple represents separation from the One True Source (see Chapter One). Adam and Eve were happy, well cared for and prospering in the Garden. When Eve took a bite from the apple, she showed doubt and fear that she was not whole and complete as she was, but that she needed something outside of herself to become powerfully expressive. So she received the opportunity to toil and grow her own food, and weed her own garden since she seemed to like control so much. We don't know if Adam and Eve whined and moaned and blamed each other or the snake, but we do know nothing was the same ever again. They did not "go softly into that good night," nor did it remain "happily ever after."

In the yin-yan, bing-bang, tit for tat life we lead, we have to find a way to honor our desires for forbidden fruit without getting booted out of our own little paradise. "What, you call my life a paradise? No way," you protest. Sorry to hear that. It sure could be! But if it isn't, then consider that perhaps you could use a little forbidden fruit. "Are you sending me to a porno shop?" you ask with wide eyes. "No, no, no," replies the Spiritual Genius. "It is merely suggested here that you have many sides, many desires, many fancies.

Don't ignore them. Spend some time with yourself and ask yourself questions, and if you don't already know the answers, then figure out what makes you hum/tick/buzz." If you know what makes you cry, then you owe it to yourself to *also* know what makes you bubble, churn, crumble, jump, hide, shine, tremble and pant. You are the one who picked the human condition to experience. Nobody made you do it. So get the most you can out of it.

Only when you know more about yourself and all of your parts, can you go about celebrating each and every facet, making sure each one gets the appropriate and acceptable attention. What if you had a part of you that liked to express itself artistically but you never gave it a chance to paint? What if another part of you liked to engage in athletic sports and games but you never let your body get up off the couch? What if hidden inside of you is a mathematical wizard but you never brought a calculator? What if you are a world-class chef but all you ever opened was a can of Chef Boyardee? What if...? The list of your unexpressed parts can be long. But it's worthwhile to find out what happens as you explore what's hidden.

You owe it to yourself to try everything that is legal, once. "But my allergies..." Oh, for crying tears! Take an antihistamine! Look in the newspaper, get out the calendar section, throw yourself directly into the stream of life and experience something fresh and new. Find out what you are "forbidding" yourself to do and go out and find a way to do it! Make jam!

You can't be a Spiritual Genius if you repress or forbid the full expression of your human nature and creative self. Appropriate expression is what sets you apart from the crowd. That's why we call it "Genius." The "Genius" always knows the right thing to do when we give it Spiritual fruit.

CHAPTER ELEVEN

Never Be Afraid of Trying New Things. Remember, Amateurs Built the Ark and Professionals Built the Titanic.

Once you have mastered getting to know yourself, including your light and dark qualities, your overt and hidden needs and the drivers behind your system, you are ready to charge full steam ahead into the Mixmaster of life. You are now officially on your shortcut to a spiritually fulfilled life.

"What?" you cry. "Not so fast!" Okay, if you haven't taken psychological profile tests and really don't have strong feedback, here are some web sites to log onto and perhaps even spend a few dollars to get an "objective view" of yourself. See yourself as others see you. Do not rely on what your family tells you. (They are always prejudiced one way or another depending on how much you annoyed them growing up and whether or not you shared your toys). Go for the objective opinion! If you think you're a smarty-pants, prove it. Take the IQ test at *IQTest.com* or take one or more of the psychological profiles tests that are offered online. Here are just a few. You can find even more selections at keyword: psychological tests.

www.queendom.com/tests.html
www.psychtests.com
www.psychweb.com/tests/psych_tests
www.2h.com
www.deltabravo.net/custody/psychtests.htm
www.mauianalysis.com
www.selfgrowth.com/test.html
www.testsplus.com
www.quincyweb.net/quincy/psychology.html

Once you have reviewed your test results you will have a better idea of how you are perceived in the world. Remember:

It is not who we are but who we are perceived to be that matters. — John F. Kennedy

Perception is important if you intend to succeed in the world of people. If you want to live underwater with the porpoises and seaweed, then you won't need to do any of this. But if you want to live, function and succeed in society, you really ought to pay close attention to how you are perceived. Your first reaction will probably be to argue with the results of the tests. That's normal. None of us enjoys being boxed into a definition or confined to a "profile." We yearn to be that unique little critter we were told we were by the "Me Generation." (Re-read Chapter Four if necessary.) So we pound our little fists and stomp our little feet and try to be "right." Hah! Do you want to be right, or do you want to be a Spiritual Genius?

"What does all this have to do with the Ark and the Titanic?" you ask with an incredulous look on your face. *Everything*! Noah was an amateur. He didn't build ships for a living. He grew grapes, or some such crop. He was awakened by a thunder clap and advised by the Great Cosmic Voice to construct an ark. He was given measurements, instructions and direction. He was required to find his own tools, and draw his own blueprint, build his own boat, and then he was ordered to stock it for the journey.

We have to do the very same thing in our lives. First, we have to recognize that the Great Cosmic Voice comes from within ourselves. We already have gathered the tools we need by getting to know ourselves, we have received instructions from the experiences of our daily lives, and now we must set the direction of our course. We aren't meant to build someone else's ship. We are meant to build our own. Like Noah, we have everything we need inside of ourselves. The hardest task is to allow those instructions to come from deep within. The Spiritual Genius says, "Ask the hard questions of yourself, seek the right tools, process the information, build the boat and then ship out with wisdom onto the seas of life."

At the very same time we are both the amateur and the professional. Some things in life we have already mastered. In other things we are still at the apprentice level. Know the difference. Determine where you are the master and be open to learning in the areas where you still have things to learn. Seeing life through "beginner's eyes" keeps you fresh and enthusiastic. Enthusiasm is the magic elixir for leading a Genius life.

CHAPTER TWELVE

The Grass May Appear to Be Greener on the Other Side of the Fence, but You Can Bet the Water Bill is Higher.

Feeling a little sorry for yourself? You think everyone else has it better/easier/richer /deeper/softer/closer/shinier/thicker/funnier than you do? Think again! Inside just about everybody walking around in the world is an insecure teenager looking for love, appreciation and a soft place to fall. You're not the only one who has the corner on "needs." When you want what somebody else has you put yourself back in the whineyard. You are giving away your personal power and your own right to happiness. You are giving it *to* someone else. You are, in essence, simultaneously applauding and resenting them for their achievements *and* not recognizing your own. Review Chapter Two. You are unique. So act it! Be the very best *you* you can be. Stop worrying about what the neighbors are doing, or what so and so is getting/winning /being/having, and concentrate on yourself. Make the best of, and the most of, what *you already have.*

There are two simple shortcuts to abundance, prosperity and success: The first one is to become completely grateful for everything you have. "But what about the dent in my fender?" you plead. I said, *everything.* "Sheesh! I don't see how I can do that. I would be lying if I were grateful for _____ or _____, or _____." Okay then, you've just tossed away your chances for true prosperity. "What are you talking about? I make a decent salary." Well, goodie for you. Don't you want even more? "Well *of course* I do!" Then read on!

Being grateful for *everything* in your life means exactly that. Without true, genuine, honest-to-gawd gratitude, you are slamming the door on real abundance. Think of it this way: If you aren't grateful for absolutely *everything* in your life and you've done this well so far, *imagine* what your life would be like if you got into a place of true gratitude for *everything*. Takes your breath away, doesn't it?

Let us use an example. A very prominent preacher from the south exhorts his congregation: "If you are living in a ramshackle place that is falling down, go to the highest and most stable part of that shack, fall down on your knees and thank the Good Lord for your bounty."

"You have *got* to be kidding," you exclaim. "A shack?" "Ah, and therein lies the secret," says The Spiritual Genius. If you can *honestly* be grateful for what you have created in your life, and *you* have created it all, then you fling open the cosmic gates for more to come in. You may have to do a lot of thinking and a lot of work to get to the place where you are truly grateful for everything in your life. *Everything!* That includes those things you perceive as the knocks as well as the glories.

"How can that be possible?" you ask. It's the paradox of prosperity, sweetie pie. First, you have to value everything you have for the *rich kingdom* it already is, and *then* you will attract an even higher level of abundance. "But I'm living in a box under the freeway, me, the box and now this damn book, " you protest. "How can I possibly be thankful for that?" Might be challenging. Still, you have to be. Be grateful, be thankful. Acknowledge your box and this book as bounty and then you will be open to receive more abundant conditions. And, it won't work if you pretend! You have to be genuine and really, really mean it. If you fake it, you'll get fake right back. You *have* to do what it takes to find that gratitude inside of yourself, no matter what it requires. Do the work! If you're not honestly grateful for what you have, you won't be able to create any more than what you have right now. In fact it may even backfire and you'll create a "bounty" of less.

The second shortcut to being wealthy and abundant is living beneath your means. I hear you screaming loudly, "Whaaaaaaaat?" Yessiree! You have to take matters into your own hands and *create* abundance in your own life to prove that you can actually handle it. Otherwise, how will the Great Source of Divine Supply know you can be trusted with more? It won't! It will only distribute as much to you as you demonstrate that you can handle. You can always have more of everything you want, you just have to prove how big a flock you can shepherd, before you are given more sheep.

"Oh no, now I have to be a goat herder," you complain. "No, no, no. It's just another one of those tedious metaphors. Let's say you knew someone was capable of looking after only so many goats or sheep before they panicked, lost them or left them alone. Would you, in your right mind, give them any more animals to tend? Of course not! You'd give them only as many sheep as you determined they could manage. And you'd make your decision based on observing how well they handled the current flock. You wouldn't be a macaroon about it, especially if you paid them per sheep. If you sent them out with ten and they came back with nine, would you really give them more when they'd already lost ten percent of your flock? You'd be a toasted macaroon if you did!

That's exactly the way abundance and prosperity work for all of us. As long as we provide the evidence that we are mentally and physically capable of handling more, we'll get it. The lesson is to take really good care of what you already have and be exceedingly, genuinely grateful for it. And then, watch what happens!

Which also means, you must live *under*, not just within your earnings (means.) If you max yourself out on credit cards, adopt debt as your first-born child and act without respect for the energetic of money, then you will find your-self always short of it. Energy is neither created nor destroyed; it merely changes form. Substitute the word "money" for energy in that phrase and you'll get the concept. Money is simply a tangible form of energy. It is a means of exchange.

We trade one thing we have for another thing we want. Humans invented "money" to symbolize that exchange. It could just as effectively be clam shells or golden walnuts. Money is merely a substantive metaphor for the energy shifted from one person or place to another. Therefore, money needs to command our respect and our honor. When respect is present, money no longer becomes something outside of us. It is a part of us and as such, deserves to be treated with great care. We don't worship money as something outside; we honor it as an extension of our own sacred life and sacred energy.

Consider for a moment what would happen if we did away with the paper and coin symbol of this energetic exchange and simply created "energy accounts." You would have your energy account and I would have mine. If I wanted something from you, an item or a service, I would simply debit my energy account. Ultimately, in order not to be overdrawn, I would have to go out into the world and put more energy back into the account through my actions or sale of goods. Depending on what I was willing to contribute, and the degree of my contribution, the level of my energetic account would increase. You might be willing to deposit more hours of a particular service than I would. Therefore, your energy account might grow faster than mine. I might come across an opportunity that you are excited to embrace, so you might be willing to contribute from your energy account to have it. Therefore my account would rise in the exchange.

It's all a system of exchange. When you lock into that concept, you will instantly see how important it is to live *beneath* your means. You always want to have a reserve store of energy to cover yourself. You can't steal energy. You can't borrow energy. You can't bilk someone else out of his or her energy. All you can do is store your energy up and exchange it for what you want. You can't always predict when you will want or need to use it.

Live beneath your means! If you are overextended, up to your eyeballs in debt, maxed out on your credit cards, then right now, today, grab yourself by the nape of the neck and say, "Stop it!" And then, *Stop It*. Before you go out for one more dinner, buy one more cup of designer coffee, collect one more handbag, or purchase one more pool toy, get a grip on your energy flow, and take control of where it goes. It's the complete opposite of weight loss. In the dynamic of weight control you output (exert) more energy and you input fewer calories. With the energy of money, by exerting or spending less (output of money) you accumulate more (inflow of money).

Confused? Probably not. More than likely you're just a little unwilling to let go of past thinking about money. "The root of all evil," so the saying goes. Money, or energy, isn't the root of anything evil, thinking is. Change the way you think about money and you will alter how it behaves in your life.

The way to change what you think about money is to play with these concepts in your head, let them swim around a bit and then open up your own energetic account. Be your own banker. Keep track of the energy you put out and watch your returns. Look at the many variations of those returns. They could be coin of the realm, they could be favors, they could be opportunities, kindnesses, compliments, services or a myriad of other avenues through which humans exchange energy with other humans. After a month of keeping track, form your own conclusions and make the changes in your life that match your desires to expend energy and experience return. By using the chart on the following pages you will quickly see how your output compares to your inflow.

(See the chart on the following pages.)

Date	Activity	EnergyType

Energy Amount	Output	Inflow

Make a notation of the *date*, describe the *activity* such as going to work, feeding the family, getting the car repaired, meditating, exercising, grocery shopping, mowing the lawn, etc. Then, determine what *type* of energy was required—mental, physical or spiritual. Then quantify how much "energy" the activity required (calculate by hours, strenuousness or whatever has meaning for you), and place a *value* on the activity by simply marking whether this was *output* or *inflow*. Going to work is output; receiving a paycheck is inflow. Paying for the movies is output; laughing your head off at the movie is inflow.

You will soon see how you spend the energy in your life and what returns you are receiving from those activities. What's the balance? How much of it is working for you? Where do you feel there is imbalance? Isn't it easier to be grateful for energy patterns rather than money as you knew it? You are beginning to loosen your mind grip on the old concept of money.

If you're not quite where you need to be yet, there are a few other things you can practice until you embody the totality of gratitude and energy banking.

Exercise: Get a blank piece of paper and complete the following

I am grateful for: _____
                                   (list ten things)

I would like to change: _____
                                   (list ten things)

I am willing to: _____
                                   (list ten things)

I am unwilling to: _____
                                   (list ten things)

I require help with: _____
                                   (list as needed)

I set the following goals: _____
                                   (list as needed)

I will achieve them by: _____
                                   (dates)

You may find that by using a positive statement daily, you will experience an increase in your energetic flow. Try this, or make up your own:

> *I am surrounded by unlimited energy all the time. The energy I put out is returned to me at least tenfold. I am deeply grateful for all that I have. I open my mind and heart to receive a continuous and generous supply of all that I can contain. This supply is abundant, ever-flowing and shared by all who claim it. I bless my supply and I am blessed in return. Thank you, Divine Prosperity (or whatever you choose to call it).*

Now then, once you have mastered this concept and the practice of energy as your form of exchange, you absolutely need to get a tight mental grip on the concept (and requirement) that you "give back" ten percent (or more!) of your inflow to the person, place or thing that inspires your life. If you collect a lot of "energy" then you *must* redistribute some of it back into the general flow. When you take water from a well, it is your responsibility to replenish the source from whence it came. You may not have to replace the water you drank, but you do need to replace the energy, to prime the pump, for the future.

Remember we are talking *energy* here. Energy, as we have said before, translates into money, time, favors, services, etc. You keep ninety percent of the intake for yourself and then you make sure you replenish your source. In your job, give back ten percent of your paycheck and time to a charity. Volunteer to assist others in gaining the knowledge and skills you have. If you make a lot of cash/energy, be sure you give back ten percent of all intake.

It makes a great deal of practical sense to reseed the forest after we have harvested the wood. Make sure you do it, or you may as well throw the first part of this chapter away. (And you've secretly been waiting for that opportunity, haven't you?) If you make a dollar, share ten cents. If you try to get around this principle, you might as well write "Home, Sweet Home" on your box under the freeway.

CHAPTER THIRTEEN

Deny Everything, Admit Nothing and Demand Proof.

At first glance this chapter title may look like a lawyer's slogan right out of a TV crime drama. You're right, it is. "But how can this have anything to do with being a Spiritual Genius?" you query. Look and see.

Deny Everything. In legal terms this means, don't give away any extra information or fall victim to what you may think is an innocent line of questioning because it may turn out to be incriminating. In a spiritual sense it means, *Deny Everything* that is outside the framework of positive thinking. Construct for yourself a consciousness and a way of thinking that affirms everything you want. By affirming what you want to think, you actually prevent being entrapped or overshadowed by another's thinking or influence. You design your own thoughts around what you want to have in your life, not what you are handed or commanded by others. "Yeah, but how do I do *that*?" you ask. You do that by speaking only positive words, thinking only positive thoughts and being eternally grateful for everything that comes across your path. You repeat daily affirmations. You offer prayers of gratitude and you instantly stop complaining.

Deny Everything that does not support your greatest good, your personal happiness and your spiritual fulfillment. You don't have to accept anything less. You *really* don't! So many of us have lived years of our lives under the mental thumb of someone else, perhaps a parent, a school, a system, a spouse or a culture. We abided by their rules because it was what we needed to do at the time for our own survival. We probably even picked up their system of thinking and believing. And here is where more real work comes in. You must examine everything you believe. Break those beliefs down one by one. Then *reassess* every belief. Start now.

Exercise:

Take a blank piece of paper, think about an area of your life that's not working as you'd like it to, and list a belief you have about this situation.

Then ask yourself:

> How does this belief serve me?
> Does this belief help or hinder me?
> Is it time to change it?
> If I change it, how will that affect my life?

If you choose to change the belief, put a positive, declarative sentence in its place and repeat it over and over until you *feel* your mind shift. Replace any and all negative beliefs with a positive statement. Here is an example:

Statement

My Belief: "Only good-looking people are successful in life."

Questions

Question: How does this belief serve me?
Answer: _____

_____

Question: Does this belief help or hinder me?
Answer: _____

_____

Question: Is it time to change it?

Answer: _____

_____

Question: If I change it, how will that affect my life?

Answer: _____

_____

The Changed Statement

"All people can be successful in their lives if they choose to be. I am successful at everything I do."

When you change your belief about a person/place/thing, you will change your life. You will draw to yourself only the positive thought and the positive energy you put out. There is nothing more important than the work you do on yourself. There is no greater investment in this lifetime than self-improvement. You bought the book, now bite the bullet, carve out the time and just do it. Change every limiting belief into a positive statement.

Admit Nothing. In a legal sense we know we ought to have an attorney present if we are being questioned. This avoids entrapment and a host of other nasty little repercussions including false imprisonment. In spiritual terms we *Admit Nothing* that doesn't contribute to our quest, daily. We let nothing into our lives that isn't supportive or encouraging. We admit only that which moves us ahead on the board game of conscious spiritual growth. "Yeah but what about my relatives?" you inquire. "Them too," says the Spiritual Genius. "I can't just catapult them out of my life," you exclaim. "There are ways," says the Spiritual Genius. "You just have to pick the highest road." (Your deep sigh is heard and registered.)

So whose life are you really living: Yours, theirs, someone else's? Make a choice. You don't have to ride them out of Dodge in a flurry of dust, but you *can* use principles and manners to get them out of your sphere of influence. You'll begin by believing there is a creative spark within you that knows the exact, perfect way to tone them down and tune them out. As you become stronger in your own Spiritual Genius, you will find the kindest ways to state the obvious.

> *You can complain because roses have thorns, or you can rejoice because thorns have roses.* — Kahlil Gibran

It's all about changing your point of view, isn't it? When the time comes to get out from under the thinking and influence of others, you will instinctively know the right way to do it. As your consciousness opens and widens, and as you practice the steps in this book, people will automatically be attracted to you. Or they will be repelled.

They will be repelled if they are lower on the consciousness scale and closed to, confused by and threatened with their own growth, or yours. If that happens, all you do is bless them where they are and gently step away. Say a prayer for them and wish them well in finding their perfect path, as you have found yours. In time, they may come forward and ask you about your path. You can certainly share what you know, but not until they ask. It comes down to age-old respect. Rest assured that it is spiritually acceptable to pray for their "highest good and farthest distance." Maybe they'll move out of town for a "better job." You'll secretly know it's all for a greater good. And, you'll be free of their influence.

It may be useful to refer to this quote:

Life is a theater. Invite your audience carefully. Not everyone is healthy enough to have a front row in the seat in our lives. There are some people that need to be loved from a distance. It's amazing what you can accomplish when you let go of, or at least minimize, your time with draining, negative, incompatible, not-going-anywhere relationships/ friendships. Observe the relationships around you. Pay attention! Which ones lift and which ones drain? Which ones encourage and which ones discourage? Which ones are on a path of growth uphill and which ones are going down? When you leave certain people do you feel better or worse? Which ones always have drama or don't really understand, know or appreciate you? The more you seek quality, respect, growth, peace of mind, love and truth around you, the easier it will become for you to decide who gets to sit in the front row and who should be moved to the balcony of your life. If you cannot change the people around you, change the people you are around. — Anonymous

Admit Nothing and no one into your life that isn't exactly what you want. Don't stay in a relationship that harms you in any way. Get out! Don't stay in a job that stifles you or diminishes you. Move on! Don't serve a master of any type that doesn't empower you, honor you, and stretch you to your greatest heights. At the end of the day, be able to look at yourself in the mirror and honestly say, "Today I moved further along my chosen path. I am wiser, happier, and more fulfilled than I was yesterday. I acted in kindness toward all and I am a success." If you can do that every night, you will watch your life expand exponentially. If you can't yet say that to yourself, then fix what may be off track, and begin fresh tomorrow.

The voyage of discovery is not in seeking new landscapes, but in having new eyes.
— Marcel Proust

Part three of this triplet is: **Demand Proof**. From a legal standpoint this statement places the burden on the law. "Show me," it says. Under the law we are "presumed innocent" until we are proven guilty. Spiritually we mean, *Demand Proof* from your experience. Take a good, hard look at what you are demonstrating in your own life. What evidence do you have to show for the quality of your life? We're not talking about how big your bank account is, how fast your car is, or how many toys you have in your toy chest. We're talking about what shows up when you do an assessment of your spiritual qualities and achievements. Anybody can purchase a sparkly, shiny, sleek, fast and groovy thing, but what is the true measure of your spiritual height? Get out your tape measure.

The Spiritual Genius says, *"Proof* is what we want. Proof that the actions of your life are positive evidence of how you think and what you believe. Proof that this lifetime of yours has a meaning deeper than the newest four-wheel drive. Proof that you have sought personal improvement and walked a spiritual path, and in walking it, have brought more joy into the world. Proof that the world around you is made better every day by your presence. Proof that the people in your past who put you down were dead wrong. Proof that no matter what the circumstances are, you always rise up victorious, positive and grateful. Proof that you can be consistently relied upon for kindness. Proof that your life is one to be cherished and admired. Provide living proof that yours is a life the next generation will want to emulate."

Demand Proof. Don't let another day go by without demanding proof from yourself. Keep asking until you get the answers you want. And then, keep on proving. No one but you can demand proof. Prove yourself *right*.

CHAPTER FOURTEEN

Turn Your Life into a Working Vacation.

Let's return full circle to my friend, Geraldine Jones. This woman will not leave me alone! For well over a year she has unceasingly hammered at me to step up and step out. She wants me to tell the world my Truth, as I know it. She told me she relies on me for Truth. I can tell you, I rely on her. She absolutely would not leave me alone until I wrote this book! Lordy! (That's how she behaves when she feels something tugging at her from way deep down inside.)

Geraldine has a very gregarious "still quiet voice" inside and she also has a powerful booming way of delivering the message once she hears it. She lives and breathes people. She is Spirit-on-a-Stick and Action Central dot com all rolled into one amazing being. She wants everybody and everything to experience life at the busting-at-the-seams level of joy she experiences every day of her life. Her word follows thought, and her deeds follow words. She thinks it up, tells you what she's going to do and then she does it. Amazing grace, she is!

Here's an example of what I mean. Last month she brought her elderly mother and mother-in-law to church. With trowels in hand, and the permission of the Minister, the three of them planted bright and beautiful annuals and perennials all around the periphery of the building because Geraldine wanted the colors of Spirit and the sacred sweetness of flowers to greet and bless everyone as they entered the church. "Don't you tell *anybody* I did it," she boldly shook her finger and admonished me. She is an active example of Ronald Reagan's familiar quote, "It's astonishing how much gets done when no one cares who gets the credit." Geraldine and her helpers not only brightened up the church, but they added a layer of kindness to the facility. The congregation may not know how it got there, but they respond to it, and that's all that matters for Geraldine. They may "think" it's the blooming flowers, but it's really the love behind them that produces the boldest and brightest colors.

Why am I telling you this? Because Geraldine

does so many things in the world anonymously. She doesn't have to; she could step out, take the credit and accept the applause, but she prefers to do it all quietly.

Years ago, Flip Wilson was in the process of creating a character for his television show and comedy routine. He was working on the comic personality of a spirited woman who takes no guff from anyone. Coincidentally, the name he had chosen was "Geraldine." Through an introduction from his manager to the real "Geraldine," he was so taken by her outspoken and over-the-top self, her outrageous loving spirit and her clever, right-on-the-money words, that they became instant friends. From that day on you couldn't tell the difference between his "Geraldine" and the real Geraldine. It was confusing even for them! Each time he dressed up in a mini-skirt, high heels, opera length pearls and waved his arms around, speaking in a sassy tone, you never knew quite who he was imitating. So much so that NBC started a national campaign, put the two of them on national television side by side, and asked the audience to guess who was the "real" Geraldine!

Here is a woman, made famous by one of America's leading comedians, a singer and performer in her own right and a vocal coach for both seasoned and rising stars, who dedicates her life's work to quietly helping and healing anybody she comes across. She could easily be lunching in fine Beverly Hills restaurants, shopping all afternoon on Rodeo Drive and leading the high life of a singing star. But she has been called by her own standards to do otherwise.

She makes her entire life a working vacation. She is always working/vacationing on something, and it's always something of her own choice, something that she decides needs to be done to make the world a better or more beautiful place. She always chooses to do it with pure joy. Not only has she repeatedly volunteered her services to perform full concerts for charity, but she's also added her name to the list of volunteers for the set up and clean up committee as well. If that isn't enough, after she rehearses for days on end and works her fanny off, she purchases extra tickets with her own money to give away to people who feel they cannot afford to attend. Those are the rules she lives by. The rules of unity, compassion, generosity and keeping your word.

As I told you before, watch out! If she sees you across the room and you look like you are not loving your life, she makes a beeline for you, hugs you up one side and down the other and shakes the blues right out of you on the spot! She can't bear to see anyone out of alignment with the greatest joys in life. So she hugs you until she darn near breaks your brittle, resistant back with love; until you cave in and surrender to her love.

Sometimes we call her Geral*damn*dine because she refuses to let anyone hide their Spiritual Genius. Geraldine is like the saying, "What you resist, persists." If you're not absolutely filled with joy in your life, then figure out a way to patch your leak and get there. Get into that state where you don't know the difference between work and vacation. Let us all strive to have a little more of Geraldine in our own lives. Be Joy on a Stick. Pretend, just for a moment, your work *is* your vacation. Pretend you *vacation* for fifty weeks a year and then *work* for two. Now doesn't that just toast your coconut?

If you aren't thrilled with what you are doing in life, then change it to something that really engages your Spiritual Genius and gets it revving on all engines all the time. If you want to make a move from where you are to "there," then the first thing you have to do is to love what you're doing right now. It's going right back to the *gratitude* concept from Chapter Twelve. To have more abundance; you must first be grateful for what you presently have. To be released from a job or situation you don't like, you first have to learn to love the one you have. When you honestly love it, you're ready to attract a better situation. Not before!

"But what if my job is a dead-end and my boss is a control freak/alcoholic/demanding /two-faced/jerk/selfish/incompetent/loser who doesn't appreciate me?" you whimper. "So what?" retorts the Spiritual Genius, "So *what*! You are not responsible for your boss, your boss's feelings, your boss's marriage or lack thereof. You are only responsible for yourself." If you arm yourself with positive thoughts, affirmative statements and you show up and do your very best every single day, that's really all you have to do. You have to use your tools to change your routine and spice up your thinking. Read the book *What You Think of Me is None of My Business* by Terry Cole-Whittaker. That'll help keep you focused on what is important and what is not. In the meantime, memorize these thirteen simple rules of life, especially for your life at work:

The Thirteen Infallible Rules
for a Great Life:

- Think quickly, speak slowly and always keep your word.
- Take nothing personally.
- Do your best at everything; always assume others are doing their best, too.
- Tell the Truth.
- The best way you can even a score is to forget it.
- Never miss a good chance to shut up.
- Trust that you have everything you need to handle every situation you are in.
- If you find yourself in a hole, quit digging.
- Don't take life too seriously; no one ever gets out alive.
- If you want to reach your dreams, don't become someone else's nightmare.
- In two days tomorrow will be yesterday.
- Always drink upstream from the herd.
- Stop looking for the keys to the Universe; it's unlocked.

CHAPTER FIFTEEN

Harmony Is More Than a Musical Term, It's the Key to Life.

Once you have done the self-examination discussed in this book, and once you have committed yourself to unleashing your Spiritual Genius, there is one more thing you need to know and achieve: harmony.

The only reason we do not experience harmony all the time is that we taint our experience with a thought, a word or a deed that is based in negativity. The negative *Thought* is that someone or something isn't perfect and unless it is changed, we can't feel good, whole or complete. The negative *Word* is what we might say about someone or something that diminishes their value and self-anoints us as the almighty, superior critic who has a right to devalue another. And the negative *Deed* is an action that is devoid of principle, self-centered or uncaring about someone or something. A negative deed can range from assault to littering as they both go against natural order and are both hostile at their core.

To live in harmony is to become congruent in what we think, what we say and how we act. The coming-together of all those elements creates happiness because we can't *be* anything but happy when we are thinking, saying and doing the things that support our good, and everyone else's.

Johann Pestalozzi says, "Man must search for what is right, and let happiness come on its own." Or as Nathaniel Hawthorne put it, "Happiness is like a butterfly which, when pursued, is always beyond your grasp, but, if you will sit down quietly, may alight upon you."

We can achieve harmony, happiness, contentment and joy and all of the qualities we wish for in life if we become congruent. As long as we are fighting "thought wars" within our own minds, we will never feel harmonious.

Key Points to remember:

- What happens *to* you is not as important as what happens *within* you.

- It's not your position in life, but your *dispo*-sition that will determine your success.

- You reveal yourself to the world by your behavior.

- Accepting that most things are difficult before they are easy alters your outlook on all things.

- The thoughts you have chosen have brought you where you are today.

- Change your thoughts and you change your actions.

- Change your actions and you are on the road to self-mastery and success.

Harmony is not all that hard to locate. Try this next exercise as an experiment with your own sense of inner harmony and state of happiness.

Exercise:

Find a tranquil place, sit quietly and think back to a moment in time when you felt really happy. Describe the quality of that experience to yourself. What were your thoughts then? Did they match your words? What were you doing? Can you identify the thread of harmony in this memory? Why were you happy? Skip down memory lane again until you can excavate another experience in which you harmoniously united thought, word and deed. Explore that feeling so you know how to easily identify it when it happens again.

Creating congruity in your life takes a willingness to run a continual check-up and check in, much like the diagnostics on a computer. This is our spiritual virus scan. We can so easily get off track when the circumstances in our lives pull us in different directions. Personal hurricanes come in all shapes and sizes. Some are like Katrina, devastating and displacing entire communities. Others are powerful storms that upset or destroy our leisure time, place or vehicle. No matter what the gale force, personal hurricanes create change. We need to stay on top of life no matter what blows into it.

Constant evaluation and reflection will keep you firmly footed on the path. Do yourself a huge favor and plan regular self-evaluation sessions of your life. Run a spiritual virus scan and keep taking inventory. Businesses do it in the first quarter of the New Year. Why not set aside the end of January each year to take an inventory of your own most important stock—your thoughts, words and deeds? Make sure they all fit together to create the harmonious life you deserve.

The goal of this book is to help you look at what you are thinking and what you believe. I never believed I could be a Spiritual Genius until someone I loved and admired told me she thought I was one. It was a humbling moment because I suddenly realized I wanted to live up to that assignment. I've worked to develop these skills over a lifetime, to achieve an inner sense of self-love and well-being, to become a contribution to society and to honor other persons, places and things. If I could learn them, so can you.

These ideas work and they are effective.

They are building blocks for a congruent life. They can be assembled in any order and they can be mastered over time. The only essential element is that you learn them, acquire the qualities they produce and live your life according to the standards that you create.

You may already have many of these skills. You may need to build up just a few more. If you think you still need some fortification, read George Weinberg's book, *Self Creation,* and follow his method of healing the inner self. His system and tools, exercises and hints put you in the driver's seat of your own life and demand of you the biggest and best you can be. Spiritual Genius is simply a distillation of these lessons, learned quickly so you can ascend to the level of a Master. Once you have accomplished this, you will have revealed your Spiritual Genius. Congratulations. Now go out there into the world and pass it on.

But what is happiness except the simple harmony between a man and the life he leads? — Albert Camus

Private Consultation is Available.

If you are truly serious about wanting a spiritually fulfilled life you can absolutely have it. You possess all the tools you need in the preceding fifteen chapters to personally achieve that result.

It takes work. It requires dedication and a fair amount of discipline. They key point to remember is to keep the fun in it. None of the work is arduous. Every step includes great joy and can be achieved through humor and practice. And, you can always book a private session with the author for more in-depth and personal assistance. Log onto www.spiritualgenius.com for details.

More Books From Dr. kac young

Feng Shui, the Easy Way

The ancient art that can change your life overnight. This is a shortcut to proven Feng Shui principles and practices which can create immediate results in your life.

21-Days to the Love of Your Life

Create the relationship of your dreams by using this proven process to attract the mate you desire. This is a powerful and successful process for the serious seeker who truly desires a soul mate and a life partner.

Dancing With the Moon

Learn how to use the natural energies of the lunar forces to orchestrate your life, your emotions and to create a deeper experience of living life at its fullest measure. Dancing With the Moon is easy to learn and simple to use. You will be enriched daily with this process.

Star Power

Create the year you want and fulfill your dreams by working with the energies of the stars and the planets. You can create the life you have always wanted by following these 12 simple steps to harness the cosmic energies that are just out there waiting for you.

Runes for Women
A Divination Tool for Today's Goddess

An ancient divination technique that reveals and utilizes the secrets of many powerful cultures. This book changes the entire perspective on the Runes and brings out the original Goddess quality of the Runic oracle.